Texas
Wildflowers

Text and photography by Richard Reynolds

FARCOUNTRY
PRESS

ACKNOWLEDGMENTS

I give special thanks to David E. Lemke, Department of Biology, Texas State University–San Marcos, who generously donated his time to oversee the correct identifications of all the wildflowers in this book. A number of other people helped in making difficult identifications of some regional wildflowers: Tom VandenBerg, Park Ranger–Interpretation, Big Bend National Park; Guy Nesom, Botanical Research Institute of Texas in Fort Worth; and A. Michael Powell, Department of Biology at Sul Ross University in Alpine. Thanks also to my son Ben, who has helped me lug heavy equipment up steep mountain trails on numerous occasions, and, as always, I thank my wife Nancy, who for more than 25 years has supported my many trips away from home, edited my writing, and provided input on a number of creative decisions.

ABOVE: Devil's head cactus
(Echinocactus horizonthalonius Lem.)
Big Bend National Park, June 1999

FACING PAGE: Bluebonnets (Lupinus texensis)
Gillespie County, April 1990

TITLE PAGE: Bluebonnets (Lupinus texensis)
Indian paintbrush (Castilleja indivisa)
Llano County, March 1994

PAGE 4: Cardinal flower (Lobelia cardinalis)
Caddo Lake, September 1991

FRONT COVER: Big Bend bluebonnets (Lupinus havardii)
Torrey yucca (Yucca torreyi)
Big Bend National Park, March 2001

BACK COVER LEFT: Indian blanket (Gaillardia pulchella)
Winecup (Callirhoe digitata)
Bluebonnets (Lupinus texensis)
Coreopsis (Coreopsis tinctoria)
Llano County, April 1997

BACK COVER RIGHT: Maximilian sunflower
(Helianthus maximiliani)
Caprock Canyons State Park, October 1990

ISBN: 1-56037-257-5
Text and Photography © 2003 by Richard Reynolds
© 2003 Farcountry Press

Created, produced, and designed in the United States. Printed in China

"Wherever I go in America, the land speaks its own language, in its own regional accent"
—LADY BIRD JOHNSON

Texas is a state with many "regional accents." With 4,834 species of plants, it is, botanically speaking, one of the most diverse states in the U.S. In *Texas Wildflowers,* photographer Richard Reynolds showcases this diversity through an array of "ecoregions" ranging from the pineywoods and bayous of East Texas to the Chihuahuan Desert of West Texas and from the prairies and cross-timbers of North Texas to the thorn-scrub of South Texas. This compelling collection of photographs reveals the beauty of Texas wildflowers both at a distance and up close—portraying with equal enthusiasm the character of the landscapes they color and the delightful details of their individual faces.

The glory of Texas wildflowers is legendary and has inspired the lives of many—most notably Lady Bird Johnson, who founded the Wildflower Center in 1982 to promote and conserve the natural beauty of wildflowers and native plants. Mrs. Johnson grew up in the East Texas pineywoods, where she developed a deep love for the flora that characterized the countryside. Familiarity with the East Texas landscape heightened her appreciation for the unique aspects of all regions of Texas—and in later travels as First Lady, for the regions of our nation. Throughout her White House years and in the decades since, she has championed and advocated the preservation of regional diversity of wildflowers and native plants.

Reynolds applies a regional focus to his wildflower photography that is not unlike the theme in *Wildflowers Across America* by Lady Bird Johnson and Carlton B. Lees, first published in 1993. This concept is even more important today than it was a decade ago. By understanding and appreciating the special character of each part of the state, we can make informed decisions about land use and reverse the careless development practices that, in the past, have destroyed so much of the irreplacable landscape. *Texas Wildflowers* vividly illustrates how precious Texas' wildflower habitat is. May its pages awaken renewed efforts to conserve and restore the beauty of wildflowers and the grandeur of the diverse regions of Texas.

Foreword

**by Robert Breunig, Ph.D.,
Executive Director,
Lady Bird Johnson
Wildflower Center**

Introduction

Photographing Texas' wildflowers has been a major part of my thirty years as a landscape photographer. While I have photographed flowers in many other states, none are as grand or as numerous as those of the Lone Star State. There are wildflowers in virtually every corner of Texas, and they bloom in every season. Every spring, from March to May, I drive an average of 6,000 miles in search of Texas' best wildflowers. Some of this mileage is on interstate highways, but most of it is on smaller farm-to-market and dusty county roads. Finding beautiful wildflowers off the beaten path, away from speeding cars and eighteen-wheelers, is one of the serendipitous perks of my profession.

The job of a nature photographer, while full of obvious rewards, is not always easy or pleasant. For every moment of exhilaration at discovering a new species of flower or stumbling upon a spectacular field of them, there are hours and even days of incessant driving and searching, frequently in vain. Fire ants, mosquitoes, wasps, ticks, snakes, sunburn, thorns, and cactus spines are but a few of the hazards of venturing into wildflower habitats. In Texas, the best times to see and photograph wildflowers are also some of the windiest, hottest, and most humid times. Any wildflower photographer will tell you that the wind seems to pick up at the moment he or she releases the shutter, and then die down as soon they're doing something else away from the camera. I have endless stories of "the ones that got away"—great wildflower shots that were impossible to get because "the wind wouldn't cooperate."

Hazards aside, there is nothing like standing in the midst of thousands of fragrant bluebonnets lilting gently in a cool spring breeze, hiking to rugged mountaintops to photograph blooming cacti perched on lofty ledges, or taking in the delicate scent of magenta-flowered cenizo blossoms after a summer rain in the chaparral.

I am not a formally trained botanist, nor is this book intended to be a field guide. Elsewhere in this book, I will list some of the many excellent technical books available. This book is a labor of love, a portfolio of some of my best wildflower images, gleaned from the thousands of transparencies I have shot over the years. I am a photographer first and an amateur scientist at best. I still struggle to remember the Latin names of the flowers I shoot, and I rely on as many as fifteen field guides to help me identify them later. My purpose in photographing Texas' wildflowers is to share, even if only in a small way, the beauty and diversity of this precious resource.

Most of the images in this book were shot from 1990–2003. Unfortunately, not every year has great wildflowers, due, in part, to Texas' legendary droughts. Every year, it seems, drought plagues one or more areas of the state. Sometimes, the Hill

Country will have a great bloom but South Texas will not, or vice-versa. In 1990, the Rio Grande Plains had the most phenomenal bloom I have ever witnessed in that part of the state, with fields of flowers blooming in places in which I had never seen so much as a single specimen. It seemed that every roadside, ditch, and field was full of primroses, bluebonnets, Indian paintbrush, winecups, and phlox. My own property on the northern fringes of the Tamaulipan Thornscrub in Medina County was covered with a carpet of flowers unlike any I had ever seen, including Huisache daisies, fleabane, prairie verbena, gaillardia, vervain, and skullcap.

Big Bend National Park was in a long-term drought during most of the 1990s and into the new millennium, as were other areas of the Trans-Pecos. In some of those years, parts of the park received less than two inches of rain. Large stands of prickly pear turned brown, withered, and died. There was not a wildflower to be seen. But the dry spell was broken temporarily by occasional rainy periods, usually in summer, the rainy season for West Texas. Summer blooms in Big Bend are frequently more spectacular than spring blooms. Large stands of prairie verbena, golden crownbeard, woolly paperflower, trailing four-o'-clock, purple ground cherry, and Gregg coldenia take over the desert floor. Magenta-flowered cenizo cover the limestone hillsides at the middle and lower elevations.

In 2001, the spring bloom followed an unusually wet fall and early winter. Widespread stands of tri-colored mustard, nama, and bladderpod began showing in early February. As the bloom progressed through February and March, desert marigold, Big Bend bluebonnets, giant daggers, and rainbow cacti joined in the show. In April, the prickly pears had one of the most extravagant blooms ever, and I counted more than five hundred blossoms on many specimens. Not far behind, cane chollas, strawberry, and claret cup cacti flowered in late-April. May saw an unprecedented agave bloom in Green Gulch, with more than seven hundred specimens sporting 10-to-15-foot-long flower spikes, *ten times more* than the previous year.

What brings about a good wildflower bloom in Texas? The factors that enter into this equation are complex and subtle at the same time. Every year, the overall bloom is different than the year before. This year may have produced more paintbrush than usual, while next year vervain or coreopsis may be favored. I used to try to predict the upcoming bloom based on the precipitation. The rule of thumb is that you need good germinating rains in September and October, some, but not too much, precipitation from November through January, and moderate and regular rains from February to May. A good freeze or two seems to make the bloom more grand.

On the other hand, with seemingly the right amounts of precipitation at the right times, the bloom is sometimes disappointing. Or, in years when there doesn't seem to have been enough precipitation, we sometimes get a good bloom. There are obviously a number of forces at work, some very subtle, in addition to precipitation levels.

A great deal of the credit for the state's magnificent wildflowers goes to the Texas Department of Transportation, which, for many decades, has distributed literally tons of wildflower seed annually along Texas roadsides. While most Texas land is now privately owned, anyone can drive down the state's many highways and see the full glory of its precious wildflowers from the comfort of their own car. For those who prefer to get out and mingle with the wildflowers, there are many state and national parks, preserves, historical sites, seashores, and forests that can be accessed at little or no cost.

I hope that this portfolio of wildflower images will foster an appreciation of the great diversity of our native flora and inspire the reader to venture out and experience Texas' wildflowers firsthand. It is also my wish that it will increase awareness of the uniqueness and fragility of our natural resources and inspire the reader to help protect and preserve our wild lands for future generations.

Panhandle-Plains

Horsemint *(Monarda citriodata)*, Woolly paperflower *(Psilostrophe tagetina)*, Indian blanket *(Gaillardia pulchella)*
Palo Duro Canyon State Park, June 1997

The northernmost sector of Texas, the Panhandle-Plains, is part of a huge mesa that occupies roughly 22 million acres in northwest Texas and eastern New Mexico. This area includes both the High Plains and Low Rolling Plains. The Llano Estacado, as it is sometimes called, is the remnant of a vast grassland prairie that once extended into Canada. Other than the shin oak, the region is virtually devoid of native trees. The region is classified as semiarid, receiving 12–21 inches of precipitation annually, the higher amounts falling in the eastern sections. Late spring and early summer provide most of the rain.

The flat-to-rolling landscape is characterized by short prairie grasses, cacti, yucca, and buffalo gourd. Thousands of playas, ephemeral shallow lakes, dot the landscape after significant precipitation. They provide habitats for aquatic plants and those that grow in moist conditions. Primary indicator plants include arrowhead plant, knotweed, and the tiny *aster subulatus*. In areas where the topsoil has eroded, underlying caliche is exposed. Despite its barren appearance, caliche supports many flowering species; bladderpod, Plains blackfoot daisy, gay feather, and broomweed are just a few.

Dramatically incising deep canyons and arroyos into the eastern edge of the Southern Plains, the canyons of the Red, Brazos, and Colorado Rivers create striking counterpoints to the flat landscape above. The walls of the steep canyons provide a vertical association of plants, with those requiring more water toward the base and those more tolerant of drier conditions toward the top. These canyons support a profusion of wildflowers, including woolly paperflower, gaillardia, basket flower, and horsemint.

RIGHT: Common sunflower *(Helianthus annuus)*
Briscoe County, June 1999

ABOVE: Purple coneflower
(Echinacea angustifolia)
Palo Duro Canyon State Park,
June 1999

LEFT: Sand verbena (Abronia
fragrans), Spotted beebalm
(Monarda punctata), Spiderwort
(Tradescantia sp.), Prickly poppy
(Argemone albiflora)
Fisher County, June 1999

FAR LEFT: Cholla cactus
(Opuntia imbricata)
Armstrong County, June 1997

ABOVE: Maximilian sunflower
(Helianthus maximiliani)
Caprock Canyons State Park, October 1990

RIGHT: Four-point evening primrose
(Oenthera rhombipetala)
Motley County, June 1997

FACING PAGE: Golden wave
(Coreopsis tinctoria)
Armstrong County, June 1997

FACING PAGE: Buffalo gourd *(Cucurbita foetidissima)*
Indian blanket *(Gaillardia pulchella)*
Woolly paperflower *(Psilostrophe tagetina)*
Armstrong County, June 1997

BELOW: Broomweed *(Gutierrezia sp.)*
Caprock Canyons State Park, June 1999

ABOVE: Horsemint *(Monarda citriodora)*
Woolly paperflower *(Psilostrophe tagetina)*
Indian blanket *(Gaillardia pulchella)*
Palo Duro Canyon State Park, June 1997

LEFT: Basket flower *(Centaurea americana)*
Dickens County, June 1999

West Texas Basin and Range Province

Ocotillo *(Fouquieria splendens)*
Big Bend National Park, April 2001

Of the four deserts in the United States, the Chihuahuan Desert is the largest, despite the fact that only thirty percent of it lies in the U.S. (the remaining seventy percent lies in Mexico). It has an extremely rich diversity of plant life—more than 1,500 species, despite an annual rainfall of only 8–20 inches. Covering 175,000 square miles, the Chihuahuan Desert in Texas lies west of a broken line extending from southeast of Del Rio to just east of the Guadalupe Mountains. The region receives so little moisture because of its location in the "rain shadow" of mountains to the west and southwest. The majority of the precipitation it receives falls during the summer monsoon season, although smaller amounts occasionally fall in the form of ice and snow in winter.

Although the dominant plant community in West Texas is comprised of small-leaved, shrubby, and often thorny plants such as creosote bush and tarbush, blooming species are abundant, due in large part to severe overgrazing by cattle in the early part of the twentieth century. Opportunistic species including mesquite, prickly pear cactus, broomweed, acacia, and yucca moved in to replace the once-lush grass.

In years when late-summer and fall precipitation is abundant, spring ushers in a diverse palette of wildflowers in Big Bend National Park. Big Bend bluebonnets, desert marigold, bladderpod, rainbow cactus, verbena, nama, and damianita put on extravagant shows. In higher elevations, mountain sage, woolly loco, claret cup cactus, agave, and wood sorrel thrive in the cooler, moister conditions.

Barrel cactus (Ferocactus wislizenii)
El Paso, September 1996

Spring is not the only time wildflowers flourish in the desert. Plentiful late-spring and summer rains bring about summer blooms that often rival spring wildflower shows. Pink windmills, purple ground-cherry, yellow trumpet flower, scarlet bouvardia, unicorn plant, and limoncillo may be found in abundance from July through September. Cenizo, a shrubby plant covered with small gray leaves, seemingly explodes overnight with purple, magenta, or pink flowers following summer thunderstorms, giving rise to its common name, barometer bush.

Perhaps the most striking blooming plants in the desert are the dozens of species of cacti. By far, the most common are prickly pears, of the genus *Opuntia*. These are the largest of Texas cacti, forming clumps up to eight feet tall and occasionally growing in impenetrable thickets. A good-sized prickly pear can be covered with literally hundreds of blossoms, ranging in color from pale yellow to orange to salmon-pink during the blooming season from March through June.

Other common genera of cacti include *Echinocereus*, characterized by one or more fleshy, ribbed stems and large, extremely showy flowers, such as the claret cups and strawberry cacti; *Mammillaria*, which includes the small, single-stemmed pincushion and nipple cacti; and *Echinocactus*, represented by the orange-flowered barrel cactus, the magenta-flowered Devil's claw, and the horse-cripplers.

Purple-tinged prickly pear
(Opuntia macrocentra)
Big Bend National Park, April 2001

Claret cup cactus
(Echinocereus
triglochidiatus),
Prickly pear
(Opuntia engelmannii
var. lindheimeri)
Amistad National
Recreation Area,
April 1992

ABOVE: Heyder nipple cactus
(Mammillaria heyderi)
Big Bend National Park, June 1999

LEFT: Torrey yucca (Yucca torreyi)
Big Bend National Park, March 2001

FAR LEFT: Cenizo (Leucophyllum frutescens)
Big Bend National Park, August 2002

ABOVE: Heyder nipple cactus
(Mammillaria heyderi)
Big Bend National Park, June 1999

RIGHT: Agave (Agave neomexicana)
Milkpea (Galactia wrightii)
Davis Mountains, August 1996

FACING PAGE: Silverlace cob cactus
(Coryphantha albicolumnaria)
Big Bend National Park, April 2001

ABOVE: Purple-tinged prickly pear
(Opuntia macrocentra)
Big Bend National Park, May 1993

RIGHT: Rainbow cactus
(Echinocereus pectinatus)
Big Bend National Park, March 2001

FACING PAGE: Agave *(Agave havardiana)*
Big Bend National Park, June 1999

LEFT: Desert willow *(Chilopsis linearis)*
Davis Mountains, June 1991

FACING PAGE: Strawberry cactus *(Echinocereus stramineus)*
Big Bend National Park, April 1996

BELOW: Long mamma cactus *(Coryphantha macromeris)*
Big Bend National Park, August 2000

FACING PAGE: Long-spined prickly pear *(Opuntia violacea)* Sotol
(Dasylirion leiophyllum)
Agave *(Agave havardiana)*
Big Bend National Park, April 2001

BELOW: Broomweed *(Gutierrezia microcephala)*
Big Bend National Park, September 1993

RIGHT: Claret cup cactus
(Echinocereus triglochidiatus)
Brewster County, April 2002

FACING PAGE: Scarlet bouvardia
(Bouvardia ternifolia)
Fort Davis National Historic Site,
August 1996

Prairies and Lakes Region

Indian paintbrush *(Castilleja indivisa)*, Sandyland bluebonnets *(Lupinus subcarnosus)*
Bastrop County, March 1999

This region encompasses the Blackland Prairies, the Post Oak Belt, and the Cross Timbers region. It stretches from southeast Texas, near Victoria, all the way to Wichita Falls, along the Oklahoma/Texas border. The land is gently rolling to nearly level. Rainfall varies from 25 to 40 inches annually. Soils range from sandy or clay loams to dark, calcareous clays interspersed with gray, sandy loams. The prairie, in its original state, was largely a grassy plain. Original prairie grasses—bluestems, sideoats grama, bunchgrass, and switchgrass—have been replaced by buffalograss and Texas grama, as well as mesquite, oak, and juniper trees, and other woody plants. But some of the original prairie wildflowers still bloom here—Texas bluebells, various primroses, silverleaf nightshade, meadow pinks, and Texas groundsel—and they often bloom in large numbers.

Indian paintbrush *(Castilleja indivisa)*
Red buckeye *(Aesculus pavia)*
Gonzales County, April 2003

Indian paintbrush *(Castilleja indivisa)*
Blue-eyed grass *(Sisyrinchium sagittiferum)*
DeWitt County, March 1998

RIGHT: Chickweed
(Minuartia drummondii),
Drummond phlox
(Phlox drummondii),
Baby blue-eyes
(Nemophila phacelioides)
Bastrop County, March 1999

FACING PAGE: Crinum lilies
(Crinum bulbispermum)
Fayette County, March 1999

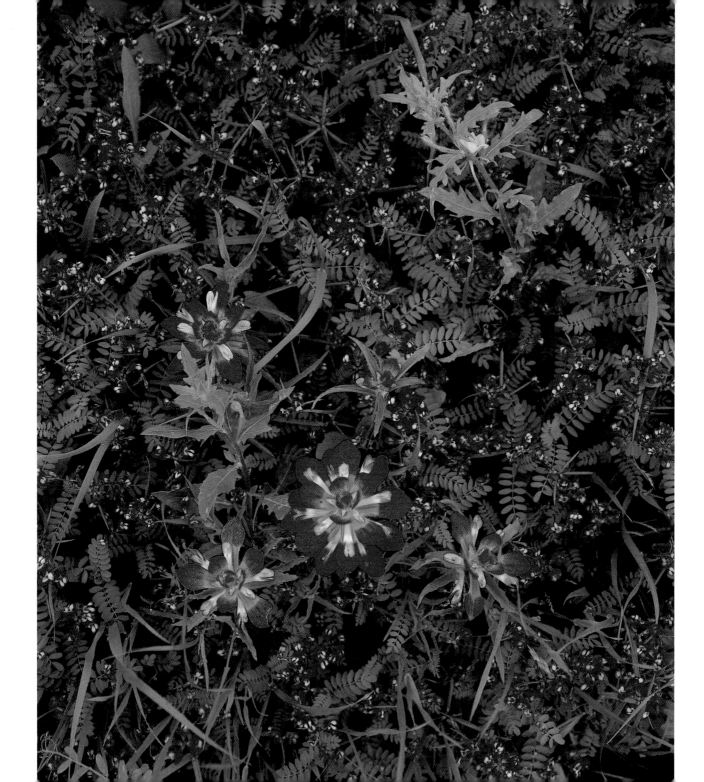

ABOVE: Drummond phlox *(Phlox drummondii)*
Baby blue-eyes *(Nemophila phacelioides)*
Gonzales County, April 2003

FACING PAGE: Indian paintbrush *(Castilleja indivisa)*
Skullcap *(Scutellaria drummondii)*
Cutleaf evening primrose *(Oenothera laciniata)*
Leon County, March 1999

ABOVE: Drummond phlox *(Phlox drummondii)*
Sandyland bluebonnets *(Lupinus subcarnosus)*
Bladderpod *(Lesquerella sp.)*
Gonzales County, April 2003

RIGHT: Red buckeye *(Aesculus pavia)*
Gonzales County, April 2003

FACING PAGE: Prickly pear *(Opuntia humifusa)*
Drummond phlox *(Phlox drummondii)*
Obedient plant *(Physostegia pulchella)*
Gonzales County, May 1997

LEFT: Indian blanket
(Gaillardia pulchella)
Medina County, April 2003

FACING PAGE: Prairie paintbrush
(Castilleja purpurea)
McLennan County, April 1997

LEFT: Rose gentian
(Sabatia campestris)
Austin County, April 2003

FAR LEFT: Bluebell gentian
(Eustoma russellianum)
Fayette County, July 1996

RIGHT: Prickly pear
(Opuntia macrorhiza)
Caldwell County,
May 1999

FAR RIGHT: Sandyland
bluebonnets
(Lupinus subcarnosus),
Huisache daisy
(Amblyolepis setigera),
Indian paintbrush
(Castilleja indivisa)
Wilson County, April 2001

FACING PAGE: Wild morning glory *(Ipomoea cordatotriloba)*
Cowpen daisy *(Verbesina encelioides)*
Dayflower *(Commelina erecta)*
Bastrop State Park, October 1998

BELOW: Pink evening primrose *(Oenothera speciosa)*
Fayette County, March 1999

Hill Country and Edwards Plateau

Prairie verbena *(Glandularia bipinnatifida)*, White prickly poppy *(Argemone albiflora)*, Bluebonnets *(Lupinus texensis)*
Blanco County, April 1997

*I*n Central Texas, an area of rugged limestone hills and deep river valleys forms the Hill Country, perhaps the most spectacular wildflower-producing area in the state. The flora of a region is usually determined by its soils, and the soils here range from dark calcareous clays to cream-colored caliche, both having evolved from the underlying Cretaceous limestone. Rainfall ranges from 10 to 15 inches in the westernmost reaches and up to 30 inches in the east.

Centered in this land of undulating hills and fertile valleys is the Llano Uplift, where igneous and metamorphic rock has pushed to the surface. The most conspicuous feature of this unusual geological area is Enchanted Rock, a huge, pink granite exfoliation dome that is one of the largest batholiths (underground rock formations uncovered by erosion) in the country.

Despite the unfertile, decayed granite soils of this area, a great variety of wildflowers thrive here. Spiderwort, bluebonnets, Indian paintbrush, greenthread, bladderpod, and basin bellflower bloom throughout the spring. Prickly pear and claret cup cacti punctuate the landscape with spectacular yellow and red blossoms respectively.

Accounts by early settlers in this region describe endless seas of wildflowers. While such vistas no longer exist, one can still encounter mile after mile of roadside flowers along most of the highways and farm roads that crisscross the area. There are still many fields and pastures, which, with adequate fall and winter moisture, will be filled with bluebonnets, prairie coneflowers, coreopsis, gaillardia, Engelmann's daisies, and brown-eyed Susans from March through June.

Giant spiderwort (*Tradescantia gigantea*)
Inks Lake State Park, March 2003

ABOVE: Texas lantana *(Lantana horrida)*
Travis County, June 1992

RIGHT: Indian blanket *(Gaillardia pulchella)*
Winecup *(Callirhoe digitata)*
Blanco County, May 1997

FACING PAGE: Indian blanket *(Gaillardia pulchella)*
Bluebonnets *(Lupinus texensis)*
Drummond phlox *(Phlox drummondii)*
Spotted beebalm *(Monarda punctata)*
Peppergrass *(Lepidium virginicum)*
Missouri primrose *(Oenthera macrocarpa)*
McCulloch County, May 1997

LEFT: Nodding thistle *(Carduus nutans)*
Kerr County, May 1995

FACING PAGE: Horsemint *(Monarda citriodata)*
Indian blanket *(Gaillardia pulchella)*
San Saba County, May 1999

ABOVE: Mexican hat *(Ratibida columnaris)*
Enchanted Rock State Natural Area, May 1999

RIGHT: Prickly pear *(Opuntia macrorhiza)*
Enchanted Rock State Natural Area, April 1994

FACING PAGE: Coreopsis *(Coreopsis tinctoria)*
Indian blanket *(Gaillardia pulchella)*
Mason County, May 1999

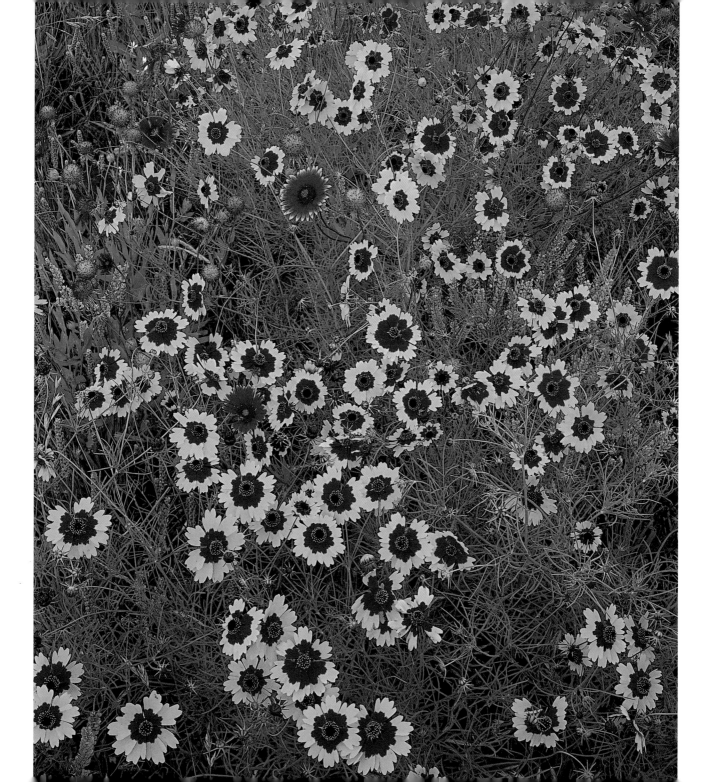

Indian blanket *(Gaillardia pulchella)*
Engelmann's daisy *(Engelmannia pinnatifida)*
Winecup *(Callirhoe digitata)*
Blue curls *(Phacelia congesta)*
McCulloch County, May 1997

South Texas and Tamaulipan Thornscrub

Strawberry cactus (*Echinocereus enneacanthus*)
Zapata County, April 1993

One of the most rugged and inaccessible parts of the state boasts some of the best wildflowers. The 11-million-acre section of Texas bordered on the east by the Gulf of Mexico and on the west by the Rio Grande, known as the South Texas Plains or Rio Grande Plains, is part of the Tamaulipan Biotic Province, most of which extends well into Mexico. The land is level-to-rolling, and ranges from sea level to around 800 feet in elevation. The region has mild winters and very hot summers. Annual rainfall ranges from 17 inches in the west to 30 inches closer to the Gulf.

South Texas boasts rich flora due to the wide variability in climate, soil types, and topography. Found here are a wide variety of wildflowers and many blooming trees, shrubs, and cacti. Early-blooming wildflowers include Drummond phlox, white and rose prickly poppies, bluebonnets, Indian paintbrush, and groundsel. Some shrubs, such as agarito, bloom in February, followed by the acacias, mimosa, and guajillo, the latter producing a light, sweet honey that is a favorite of many South Texans. Fragrant huisache trees explode with deep-yellow, ball-shaped flowers and sometimes bloom en masse as far as the eye can see.

In April, many of the mid-season bloomers—gaillardia, pink evening primrose, winecups, Huisache daisies, and blue curls—begin to show. Retama, guayacan, mesquite, and paloverde trees also begin to flower. By May, the temperatures regularly soar into the 90s, and the spring wildflower season begins to wind down.

RIGHT: Strawberry cactus (*Echinocereus enneacanthus*) Frio County, April 1991

ABOVE: Prickly poppy *(Argemone sanguinea)*
Atascosa County, April 2003

RIGHT: Prickly poppy *(Argemone sanguinea)*
Atascosa County, March 1990

FACING PAGE: Prickly poppy *(Argemone sanguinea)*
Honey mesquite tree *(Prosopis glandulosa)*
Atascosa County, March 1990

RIGHT: Blue curls *(Phacelia congesta)*
Indian paintbrush *(Castilleja indivisa)*
Medina County, April 2003

FACING PAGE: Blue curls *(Phacelia congesta)*
Frio County, May 1998

ABOVE: Indian blanket *(Gaillardia pulchella)*
Frio County, April 2003

LEFT: Indian blanket *(Gaillardia pulchella)*
Engelmann's daisy *(Engelmannia pinnatifida)*
Spotted beebalm *(Monarda punctata)*
Medina County, April 1991

ABOVE: Huisache daisy *(Amblyolepis setigera)*
Medina County, April 2003

RIGHT: Brown-eyed Susan *(Rudbeckia hirta)*
Medina County, April 2003

FACING PAGE: Tickseed *(Coreopsis nuecensis)*
Drummond phlox *(Phlox drummondii)*
Atascosa County, April 2003

ABOVE: Drummond phlox *(Phlox drummondii)*
Yellow sweet clover *(Melilotus officinalis)*
Medina County, April 2003

RIGHT: Lazy daisy *(Aphanostephus skirrhobasis)*
Drummond phlox *(Phlox drummondii)*
Medina County, April 2003

FACING PAGE: Prairie verbena *(Glandularia bipinnatifida)*
Medina County, April 1997

LEFT: Tickseed *(Coreopsis nuecensis)*
Drummond phlox *(Phlox drummondii)*
Atascosa County, April 2003

FACING PAGE: Greenthread *(Thelesperma filifolium)*
Indian blanket *(Gaillardia pulchella)*
Antelope horns *(Asclepias asperula)*
Medina County, April 1991

Gulf Coast and Coastal Prairies

Silverleaf sunflower *(Helianthus argophyllus)*, Rio Grande phlox *(Phlox glabriflora)*
Mustang Island, May 1997

First-time visitors to the Texas Gulf Coast may see only the relentless surf and miles of low sand dunes at first glance. It may appear to be a barren place until one ventures into and beyond the dunes and marshes, where a variety of plants thrive. At least 700 species of flowering plants have been found growing along Texas' 624-mile coastline.

Precipitation along the coast is heavier the farther north one goes. Rainfall amounts range from 20 inches annually along the lower Gulf Coast to 50 or more inches closer to Louisiana, most of which falls during the hurricane season from June to November. The soils of the Gulf Coast are usually sand mixed with varying amounts of clay. Soils of the broader islands tend to be less saline and have more organic matter mixed in. Sunflowers, lantana, phlox, goldenrod, toadflax, aster, palafoxia, and mist-flowers thrive here.

Dunes are usually composed entirely of sand. The deep-rooting goat-foot morning glory vine is essential in helping stabilize them. The hardy vines have been known to grow almost 10 inches per day with adequate rainfall. Not far behind in sheer number are the beach morning glories, which sometimes cover the dunes with three-inch-wide white blossoms, and the yellow-flowered beach evening primroses. Less abundant but still plentiful species making their homes on the sand dunes are purslane and cenicilla, low-growing succulents that bloom almost year-round.

ABOVE: Giant blue iris *(Iris sp.)*
Anahuac National Wildlife Refuge, April 2003

LEFT: Lantana *(Lantana sp.)*
Galveston Island State Park, April 2003

LEFT: False dragonhead *(Physostegia pulchella)*
Brazoria County, April 2003

FACING PAGE: Goat-foot morning glories
(Ipomoea pes-caprae subs. *brasiliensis)*
Padre Island National Seashore, July 1996

RIGHT: Yellow wild indigo
(Baptisia sphaerocarpa)
Anahuac National Wildlife Refuge,
April 2003

FACING PAGE: Goldenrod
(Solidago canadensis)
Chambers County, October 1990

LEFT: Spider lilies
(Hymenocallis liriosme)
Chambers County, April 2003

FACING PAGE: Lazy daisy *(Aphanostephus skirrhobasis* var. *thalassius),*
Goldenrod *(Solidago canadensis)*
McFaddin National Wildlife Refuge,
October 1990

East Texas Pineywoods

LEFT: Purple vetch *(Vicia villosa)*
Sabine County, April 2003

BELOW: Coreopsis *(Coreopsis lanceolata)*
Sabine County, April 2003

The East Texas Pineywoods are part of a vast forest that covers the southern United States from the Atlantic Ocean to Texas. This forest extends into Texas from the east some 75 to 125 miles. The terrain is rolling and often hilly, with elevations ranging from 50 to around 500 feet above sea level. Forty to 60 inches of rain fall on the region annually, and many streams, creeks, and bayous drain the region. Pine trees dominate the forested areas, but many hardwoods flourish as well, including elm, hickory, sweet and black gums, magnolia, maple, tupelo, dogwood, and a variety of oaks.

East Texas has undergone some major changes in the last 100 years. Logging and clear-cutting practices in the first half of the twentieth century removed almost all of the old-growth timber and destroyed many of the plant associations that were the heart and soul of the southern forest. To add insult to injury, much of the re-growth was subsequently cleared for farming and ranching. In 1984, Congressman John Bryant and Senator Lloyd Bentsen were instrumental in designating five substantial wilderness areas in the Pineywoods that preserve the biodiversity of the forests as they were before twentieth-century man cut a wide swath through the area. These areas lie within the four national forests that have been designated in East Texas: Davy Crockett, Sabine, Angelina, and Sam Houston. Ephemeral plant communities, which include green rein, southern twayblade, the rare yellow lady's-slipper orchids, spotted-leaf trillium, Walter's violet, and Carolina jessamine, have developed in these forested areas to take advantage of sunlight before it is blocked by leaf growth. As soon as the trees are covered by foliage, the ephemeral community fades.

RIGHT: Butterfly weed *(Asclepias tuberosa)*
Harrison County, July 2002

The Big Thicket National Preserve, in the southern half of East Texas, was established in 1974. The first preserve in the National Park System, The Big Thicket consists of nine land units and six water corridors encompassing more than 97,000 acres, protecting an area of rich biological diversity. A convergence of ecosystems occurred here during the last Ice Age. It brought together, in one geographical location, the eastern hardwood forests, the gulf coastal plains, and the midwest prairies. A number of exotic wildflowers inhabit the area—bearded grass pink, spring coral-root, green adder's mouth, and giant ladies' tresses, as well several carnivorous plants—sundews, bladderworts, butterworts, and pitcher plants.

The Big Thicket is truly a microcosm of the Lone Star State. Texas' diverse ecosystems contain an astonishing number of native organisms. It is true that much of the state has been developed and true wilderness areas no longer exist, save for a few places in the western and eastern parts of the state. Cities, farmland, and industrial areas now break up the state like a patchwork quilt. But tough and persistent creatures have learned to survive in the remaining wild lands by making the most of the resources nature has to offer. Beauty and serenity are still here. Take the time to look, listen, and breathe in the wonders of Texas' many natural treasures, including its incredible array of wildflowers.

RIGHT: American lotus (Nelumbo lutea)
Caddo Lake, July 1992

FACING PAGE: Coreopsis (Coreopsis lanceolata)
Sensitive briar (Mimosa nuttallii)
Cass County, May 2002

FACING PAGE: Sensitive briar *(Mimosa nuttallii)*
Spiderwort *(Tradescantia occidentalis)*
Camp County, April 1991

RIGHT: Crimson clover *(Trifolium incarnatum)*
Houston County, April 1991

BELOW: Coral honeysuckle *(Lonicera sempervirens)*
Sabine County, April 2003

FOLLOWING PAGE: Goat-foot morning glory
(Ipomoea pes-caprae subs. *brasiliensis)*
Padre Island National Seashore, July 1996

When and Where to See Texas Wildflowers

A good wildflower bloom begins with adequate precipitation in September and October, some, but not too much, from November to January, and then some good soaking rains in February and March. The earliest flowers to bloom in Texas will be in Big Bend National Park, sometimes starting down in the lower desert and in the canyons of the Rio Grande as early as January. The bloom will improve through February and peak in late-March, when the cactus take over, beginning with the little rainbows and brown-flowered cacti, followed closely by the prickly pears. The pears will often bloom into June, depending on the species. In mid-April, the strawberry cacti will begin to open out in the desert, and by late-April, the claret cups will begin showing up in the mountains and surrounding foothills. Agaves will peak in May and sometimes flower well into June.

The Panhandle Plains bloom is from late-April to late-June and features woolly paperflower, gaillardia, horsemint, basket flower, Mexican hat, four-point evening primrose, blackfoot daisy, greenthread, globemallow, sand verbena, and the common sunflower.

My favorite wildflower-viewing locations in the **Panhandle-Plains:**

> Palo Duro Canyon State Park
>   and Caprock Canyons State Park
> Lake Meredith National Recreation Area
> Highway 70 between Spur and Turkey
> Highway 83 from Aspermont to Shamrock
> Highway 207 between Silverton and Conway

Almost any road in the Pineywoods of East Texas has good wildflowers in April and May. Some of the more common bloomers include dogwood, honeysuckle, coreopsis, crimson clover, winter vetch, phlox, sensitive briar, and Indian paintbrush.

My favorite wildflower-viewing locations in **East Texas:**

> Highway 259 between Daingerfield and Nacogdoches
> Highway 59 between Texarkana and Center

The triangle connecting Hughes Springs, Avinger, and
  Linden, connected by Highway 155, Highway 11, and
  Highway 49 (Wildflower Trails of Texas)
Highway 190 between Huntsville and Jasper

The foothills and mountains of West Texas, including Big
Bend National Park, offer many unique and beautiful wildflowers, including Big Bend bluebonnets, desert marigold, bi-color
mustard, purple mat, scarlet bouvardia, yellow trumpetflower,
agave, cholla cactus, prairie verbena, Devil's claw, silverleaf
nightshade, and dalea.
My favorite wildflower-viewing locations in **West Texas:**
  Big Bend National Park, especially the Maxwell Scenic
    Drive and the road between Panther Junction and
    Persimmon Gap and between Panther Junction and
    Rio Grande Village
  River Road (Highway 170) between Lajitas and Redford
  Davis Mountains scenic loop drive (Highways 118 and 166)

Some original prairie flowers still bloom in the Prairies and
Lakes Region, including Texas bluebells, silverleaf nightshade,
meadow pinks, and Texas groundsel.
My favorite wildflower-viewing locations in the **Prairies and
Lakes Region:**
  Ellis, Kaufman, Navarro, and Washington Counties,
    especially in and around Ennis, Brenham, Chappell
    Hill, and Independence
  Highway 77 from Victoria to LaGrange
  Highway 79 from Round Rock to Palestine
  Highway 90 between Luling and Eagle Lake

Central Texas, which includes the Hill Country, the Edwards
Plateau, and the westernmost sections of the Blackland Prairies,
can have grand displays of wildflowers. Some of the largest
stands of bluebonnets in the entire state may be found in the

Hill Country. They begin blooming as early as late-February but
usually don't peak until mid-April. As spectacular as the blue-
bonnets are, I feel the best time for wildflowers in the Hill
Country is actually late-April into May, and occasionally even
into June, when the coreopsis, gaillardia, winecups, Engelmann's
daisies, spotted beebalm, Indian paintbrush, and prickly pear
make their presence known.
My favorite wildflower-viewing locations in **Central Texas:**
  Highway 71 between Spicewood and Brady
  Highway 16 between Kerrville and San Saba
  Highway 29 between Mason and Liberty
  Highway 281 between San Antonio and Burnet
  Colorado Bend, Inks Lake, Lyndon B. Johnson, and
    McKinney Falls State Parks
  Enchanted Rock State Natural Area

South Texas has some of the state's best wildflowers, year in
and year out. Beginning in early March in the Rio Grande Valley,
the bloom works its way northward a few miles per day. In gen-
eral, south of Highway 90 (the dividing line between South and
Central Texas), the flowers will peak in late-March or early
April. With good rains continuing into spring, the bloom period
may be extended a few weeks. Flowers to look for include bluebonnets, Indian paintbrush, gaillardia, Drummond phlox,
winecups, rose and white prickly poppies, blue-eyed grass,
groundsel, pink evening primrose, slender vervain, prairie
verbena, tickseed coreopsis, yellow flax, and Huisache daisies.
My favorite wildflower-viewing locations in **South Texas:**
  Highway 183 between Lockhart and Goliad
  Highway 97 between Gonzales and Pleasanton
  Alt. 77 from just north of Cuero to Hallettsville
  Interstate 37 between San Antonio and Corpus Christi
  Choke Canyon State Park near Three Rivers, Palmetto
    State Park south of Luling, Lake Corpus Christi State
    Park near Mathis, and Goliad State Park in Goliad

The Texas Gulf Coast and coastal prairies are excellent places to see wildflowers. The sand dunes, tidal flats, and marshes support a variety of blooming plants, including goat-foot daisies, beach morning glories, beach evening primroses, gaillardia, goldenrod, purslane, glasswort, sea oxeye daisy, and prickly pear.

My favorite wildflower-viewing locations along the

Texas Gulf Coast:

Padre Island National Seashore, a 70-mile section of the longest undeveloped barrier island in the world, with 130,454 acres of beautiful beaches, sand dunes, ponds, marshes, and tidal flats supporting 75 plant families composed of four hundred species.

National Wildlife Refuges excel as habitats for hundreds of species of birds, reptiles, and mammals, and they are also prime areas for a multitude of wildflowers and native grasses and plants. Laguna Atascosa (north of Brownsville); Aransas (north of Corpus Christi); Big Boggy, Brazoria and San Bernard (all within an hour's drive of Houston and Galveston); and Anahuac, McFaddin, and Texas Point (south of Beaumont) are good wildflower-viewing spots.

Mustang Island, Goose Island, Galveston Island, and Sea Rim State Parks offer excellent recreational opportunities as well as excellent sites to observe and photograph many species of native grasses and wildflowers.

RIGHT: Bluebonnets *(Lupinus texensis)*
Indian paintbrush *(Castilleja indivisa)*
Peppergrass *(Lepidum virginicum)*
Llano County, April 1997

FACING PAGE: Giant blue iris *(Iris sp.)*
Anahuac National Wildlife Refuge, April 2003

*T*ripod: Nothing is more true than the old dictum, "Use a tripod." Camera movement is one of the two top reasons for blurry pictures, right after wind. Think of the tripod as the foundation for good wildflower photography. It is especially important for closeups.

Lighting: Probably one of the biggest pitfalls in wildflower photography is shooting in the wrong kind of light. Direct sunlight is harsh—it creates black areas with little or no detail in the shadow areas of your film. Try to shoot on overcast, misty, or cloudy days to eliminate this problem. If you must shoot on sunny days, you can use a white sheet, white plastic, sailcloth, or other fabric to diffuse the harsh sunlight. Or, if you can invest fifty dollars or so, purchase a portable diffuser from your local camera store. They are lightweight and fold up very small.

Wind: Wind is the curse of the wildflower photographer. Unfortunately, the wildflower season is also the windiest time of year in Texas. Check your weather forecast before you go out. If the winds are predicted to be less than 15 miles-per-hour, there will probably be enough lulls to get some photos. You must have patience, and you have to be ready when the wind calms down. You can also make a small, tent-like enclosure out of the same material you use for a light diffuser. One technique that works well for some photographers is to make a large 4-by-5-foot rectangle of diffusion material and drape one end of it over your back (you will be in a kneeling or crouching position). Drape the other end over two sticks impaled in the ground behind the subject, and you're ready to shoot. I personally use large, homemade diffusers, 36 inches by 48 inches or so, which my wife made from sheets of rip-stop nylon, with elastic sewn on diagonally at each corner. I stretch it over a frame made with lightweight PVC pipe, which is available at home improvement stores.

Equipment: A 35mm camera with a 50 mm or longer macro lens is ideal for wildflower closeups. A longer focal length macro lens allows you to shoot a little farther away from your subject. This will prevent you from blocking the light by being too close

Tips for Wildflower Photography

to it. Avoid screw-in, filter-type closeup lenses if you can. They are notoriously unsharp. A better solution is to purchase extension tubes for your normal lens if you can't afford a macro lens. Since they have no glass elements, they allow you to shoot closeups without degrading the optical quality of your lens.

For more information on Texas wildflowers, visit these Web sites:

Texas Dept. of Transportation flower reports
www.dot.state.tx.us/wflwr/main.htm

State parks wildflower reports
www.tpwd.state.tx.us/park/wildflower/

Lady Bird Johnson Wildflower Center
www.wildflower.org

Big Bend wildflower reports
www.desertusa.com/wildflo/tx.html
www.nps.gov/bibe/home.htm

Texas Highways wildflower reports
www.texashighways.com

Texas wildflower sightings
http://lnstar.com/wildflowers/sightings.htm

**City of Ennis, "The Bluebonnet City of Texas,"
Convention and Visitors Bureau**
www.visitennis.org

Strawberry cactus *(Echinocereus enneacanthus)*
Chihuahua Woods Preserve, March 2000

References

Ajilvsgi, Geyata. *Wildflowers of Texas.* Fredericksburg, TX: Shearer Publishing, 1984.

Drawe, D. Lynn. and James H. Everitt. *Trees, Shrubs and Cacti of South Texas.* Lubbock, TX: Texas Tech University Press, 1993.

Enquist, Marshall. *Wildflowers of the Texas Hill Country.* Austin, TX: Lone Star Botanical, 1987.

Fritz, Edward C. *Realms of Beauty, The Wilderness Areas of East Texas.* Austin, TX: University of Texas Press, 1986.

Kirkpatrick, Zoe Merriman. *Wildflowers of the Western Plains.* Austin, TX: University of Texas Press, 1992.

Loughmiller, Campbell and Lynn. *Texas Wildflowers.* Austin, TX: University of Texas Press, 1984.

MacMahon, James A. *The Audubon Society Nature Guides: Deserts.* New York: Chanticleer Press, 1985.

Richardson, Alfred. *Wildflowers and Other Plants of Texas Beaches and Islands.* Austin, TX: University of Texas Press, 2002.

Rickett, Harold William. *Wildflowers of the United States: Texas.* New York: McGraw-Hill Book Company, 1969.

Rose, Francis L. and Russell W. Strandtmann. *Wildflowers of the Llano Estacado.* Dallas, TX: Taylor Publishing Co, 1986.

Tull, Delena and George Oxford Miller. *A Field Guide to Wildflowers, Trees and Shrubs of Texas.* Houston, TX: Gulf Publishing, 1991.

Spotted beebalm *(Monarda punctata)*
Medina County, April 2003

Warnock, Barton H. *Wildflowers of the Big Bend Country, Texas.* Alpine, TX: Sul Ross State University, 1970.

——. *Wildflowers of the Guadalupe Mountains and the Sand Dune Country, Texas.* Alpine, TX: Sul Ross State University, 1974.

——. *Wildflowers of the Davis Mountains and the Marathon Basin, Texas.* Alpine, TX: Sul Ross State University, 1977.

Weniger, Del. *Cacti of Texas and Neighboring States.* Austin, TX: University of Texas Press, 1984.

West, Steve. *Northern Chihuahuan Desert Wildflowers.* Helena, MT: Falcon Publishing, 2000.

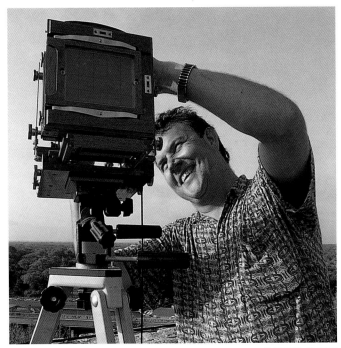

Richard Reynolds

Born in Alice, Texas, Richard Reynolds grew up in San Antonio on the fringes of the South Texas Brush Country. He now lives in Austin with his wife, Nancy, and son, Ben. Richard's involvement with photography began in 1968 during a trip to Big Bend National Park with a borrowed Kodak Signet 35mm camera. A few years later, after seeing some of Ansel Adams' luxurious black and white prints, he decided to pursue photography as a career, and he went on to receive a degree in Industrial Photography and Color Technology at the prestigious Brooks Institute of Photography in Santa Barbara, California. Initially photographing exclusively in black and white, he switched over to color in 1979 after seeing the pioneering large-format color landscape work of Eliot Porter. Following a seven-year stint as chief photographer for the Texas Tourist Development Agency and the Texas Department of Commerce, he began freelancing in 1990, specializing in landscapes of Texas and the Southwest. His photographs have appeared in numerous state, national, and international publications including *National Geographic Traveler, Newsweek, Outside Magazine, Texas Monthly, Readers Digest, Southern Living, Vista, Geo* (France), and *Richtig Reisen Texas.* He is a regular contributor to *Texas Highways,* where he has more than twenty-five covers to his credit. In addition, his work has appeared in dozens of calendars by Sierra Club, Westcliffe Publishers, Brown Trout, Golden Turtle, and Shearson Publishing. He is also the photographer of six other books: *The Green Pastures Cookbook; Texas, Images of Wildness; Texas Reflections; Texas Wildflowers; Texas Hill Country;* and *A Texas Christmas.*